UNLOCKING THE POWERS OF YOUR BELIEFS

JUDE OKEY DIKE

GRACE L. SAMSON (Ph.D)

CONTENTS

Cover design by: Andrew C. Worthy
(+2348134153193)
andresdigno@gmail.com

ACKNOWLEDGEMENTS

I thank God Almighty for giving me the wisdom, inspiration and insight to write this book. I want to thank my wife, children and siblings for their assistance and prayers.

Again, I acknowledge the wonderful assistance I got from my darling sister, Dr. Grace L. Samson who gave me the push to write this book. She is very wonderful.

Above all, I appreciate the reviewer of this book, Mr. Andrew Worthy, Dr Egbepalu Purissima and the men of God in my life: Bishop E. C. Obiora, Pastor Kola Raph and Pastor Isaac Abioye. I also appreciate Pastor Mrs Peace Obiorah for her assistance and ideas given to me freely.

Finally, I want to thank Prof. Collis Nwaogwugwu for his contribution.

Thank you all.

DEDICATION

I wish to dedicate this book to my lovely wife and children. They have been a source of support to me throughout the period I took to write this book.

To God almighty for his enablement, grace and favour.

FOREWORD

This noble work introduces the general reader into the world of BELIEF in a very simple, concise, and readable manner. The authors tried to demonstrate that we are what we think. they offer rudimentary keys to excel in life by simple acts of constructive beliefs, appropriate plans, and their executions.

Particularly interesting is their style of writing that brought about the interplay of philosophy, spirituality, and psychology, considering the fact that man is an integral being. It is an inward journey guided by faith and reason. It is a clarion call to success, by understanding how beliefs are formed, the extent to which we are influenced by what we believe in and the consequences of positive and negative beliefs.

Today's experiences invite everyone, but especially the young minds, to grasp how to build their lives towards greater authentic achievements. It is a hidden treasure. No one who discovers it dares to lose it.

Egbekpalu Purissima Emelda (PhD)

Unlocking The Powers of Your Beliefs deals extensively with the subject of belief. Using very practical examples, the authors elucidate the human belief system as being an indispensable element for a meaningful existence. According to them, a person's beliefs determine his destiny, as form the foundation of the person's existence.

Having read this brilliant piece myself, I am bold to say that the authors have a profound, exceptional knowledge in this subject area, which I believe they must have garnered from their years of experience.

With twelve chapters on different aspects of belief, and several practical theories related to it, the book deals extensively on the matter of belief, as it relates to human productivity.

This book will transform your belief system from whatever level it is at the moment to at least a 95% level. It is an eye-opener, as it has thrown more enlightenment to me on how to harness the potentials of my belief system, to achieve great success in life. The exposition in this book is truly unbelievable and I implore you to read it till the end, so that you too can transform your life by transforming your belief.

Samson Mpueh (PhD)

Wisdom-4-Excellence Books--
THE PRAYERS THAT RUN: IS IT FAITH OR FEAR (*TPTR*)?

Wisdom-4-Excellence Books--
POVERTY IS A MAN (*PIAM*)?

Read our books here
https://gracelsamson.blogspot.com/

INTRODUCTION

Do you believe in something? The answer is a resounding yes! Even the atheist believes in something. Our beliefs rule our lives. Usually, when you board a taxi, you believe the driver is a good driver even when you have not met him before. You also believe that the vehicle will not breakdown in the middle of the road. When you enter a restaurant to eat, you believe that the food is good for human consumption. When you open up a bottle of soft drink to gulp, you believe that there is no cockroach inside it. The examples are indefinite.

One indubitable fact in life is that each of us has a set of beliefs that secretly molds and controls our lives. This set of beliefs greatly affects our daily thoughts and functioning, which consequently influences our emotions. Our emotions in turn affect our behaviours and lifestyles; our lifestyles affect our achievements and destinies.

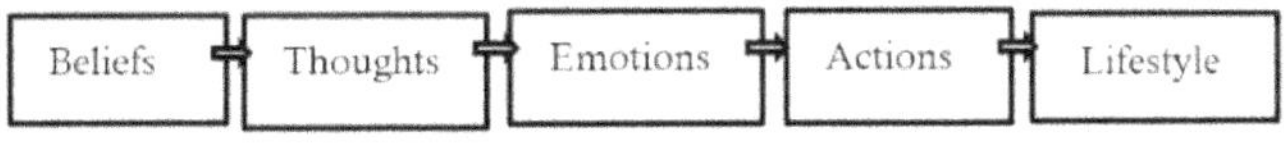

One can say incontrovertibly that our beliefs make us slaves throughout our lives. This is simply because our frame of beliefs becomes a set of instructions that governs our lives. It guides our destiny by determining how successful and happy we can be in life.

Our belief patterns are like operating systems (as in computers) in our subconscious mind, which control us daily. Oftentimes, we may not be aware that we are being manipulated by our beliefs. But they help us to cognitively appraise and analyze what we perceive. Such evaluations can be positively or negatively done, depending on our individual belief systems. In other words, our interpretations of life's phenomena depend on our beliefs. For the fact that we believe differently, we can perceive a situation as good, neutral, or bad, depending on our belief make-up.

The caveat is – beware of your beliefs! Question your beliefs. Are your beliefs life-enhancing or destructive? We shall discuss all these issues in subsequent chapters. It is heart-rending to note that negative beliefs have destroyed lives and destinies. We need to urgently recognize their effects in our lives. Consequently, we can change our lives tremendously for good if we change our beliefs.

Belief is very powerful and must be managed with a lot of circumspection. Millions of individuals all over the world have lived unfulfilled lives because of the wrong set of beliefs that they have imbibed from childhood.

This book, "Unlocking the Powers of Your Beliefs," makes attempts to explain what belief is and how beliefs are formed. The book also encourages us to believe in ourselves.

Most importantly, it explains how beliefs affect our lives and basically how we can reprogram our beliefs for success.

In summary, reading this book will help the reader achieve the following:

- To know the negative expressions that help form negative beliefs.
- To discern the differences between positive and negative beliefs.
- To know why some people are enslaved by negative beliefs throughout their lives.
- To understand how negative or non-beneficial beliefs lead to poor performance in life.
- To achieve success with ease, with the right kind of belief.
- To improve success in our daily endeavours, by having belief in our abilities.
- To believe in God Almighty who controls the universe.
- To increase our staying power when we face difficulties.
- To enable us to interpret the events of life in their proper perspective.
- To tap the energy inherent in our beliefs.

This book is titled *Unlocking The Powers of Your Beliefs* because of the need to address the issue of negative beliefs prevalent in our generation. Remember what Christ said in John 14:1 - *"let not your hearts be troubled. Believe God and believe in me"*.

This book is a clarion call to constructive beliefs. It will inspire billions of people not to allow their beliefs to work against them. It is a rare treasure, a pearl.

CHAPTER ONE: WHAT IS BELIEF?

"Believe something and the universe is on its way to being changed, because you've changed, by believing. Once you've changed, other things start to follow. Isn't that the way it works?"

Diane Duane

There are many definitions of this important term called *"belief"*. The Collins Dictionary defines it as *"the feeling of certainty that something exists, is true or is good"*. According to the Collins Dictionary, belief implies mental acceptance of something as true, even though absolute certainty may be absent.

For Wikipedia, belief is *"the state of mind in which a person thinks something to be the case, with or without there being empirical evidence to prove that something is the case with factual certainty"*. Another way of defining belief is that it is a mental presentation of an attitude, positively orientated towards the likelihood of something being true.

Remember the warning by Deepak Chopra – *"our beliefs shape our lives"*. Yes! They do. In the same way, Kola

Raph articulates that *"what you don't believe on cannot work for you"*. Explaining further, Anton Chekhov states that *"Man is what he believes."*

Life is beautiful. Planet Earth was delicately prepared for humans and animals to enjoy to the fullest. You were created to enjoy life, to excel, have wonderful family, relationships and all the luxuries of the world. You were created to work hard and enjoy the fruits of your labour, completely. You were created to have good and sound health, thriving businesses and good home, cars, children, spouse and those things that make life sweet and refreshing. However, the big challenge is **your belief.**

Your belief can hinder you from enjoying the sweetness of life. Your belief can repel the good things of life, instead of attracting them to you. Beliefs can cause great dangers if not checked. Consequently, we must change our lives positively by changing our old, worn-out, delimiting, and debilitating beliefs.

WHY DOES EVERYBODY BELIEVE IN SOMETHING?

We all believe in several things in life – whether spiritual, non-spiritual or even superstitious – that so powerfully influence and shape our lives. Even the so-called atheists who do not believe in the Almighty Creator still believe in one thing or the other.

Several countries enshrine *Freedom of Association and Belief* as part of their constitutions. Some people believe in their religious leaders, while some others believe what their computer can do for them, in science and humanity. A quick look at what people believe in would suffice to show that everybody believes in something on Earth. I need to stress that belief is not only and necessarily considered spiritual.

WHAT PEOPLE BELIEVE IN AROUND THE WORLD

People around the world believe in the following:

GOD ALMIGHTY – God Almighty is the creator of the cosmos and everything therein. As a matter of fact, many names are gotten from the names of different gods. We got our calendar from the names of some Roman gods. An example is January (Janus – the god of new beginning).

A few other things that people believe in are:

- Black Magic (Juju)
- Reincarnation
- Luck
- Superstition
- Fatalism - Every action or event has been pre-determined to happen.
- Spiritual manipulation
- Astral travels
- Fellow human beings/humanity

- [ ] Sports
- [ ] Universal laws
- [ ] Constitutions
- [ ] Sorcery
- [ ] Science
- [ ] Destiny
- [ ] Heavenly bodies – sun, moon, and stars

Carolyn Spring has this to say – *"as a child, the best way to survive was to be still, to submit; to do nothing that might incur further harm. That belief had grown with me through my teens, my twenties, my thirties, are unacknowledged mentor directing my every faith, reinforcing a ubiquitous sense of powerlessness and victimhood. I had believed that I was bad and unlovable, coward, and weak. These beliefs have been unconscious in me and had always gone unchallenged. I believed them because they were true and because I believed them to be true."*

CHAPTER TWO: HOW BELIEFS ARE FORMED

"Be not afraid of life. Believe that life is worth living and your belief will help create the facts."

Prof. William James

Beliefs come primarily from our environment, religious leaders, parents, personal experiences; the books we read and persons we meet every day. After the birth of a child, the mind of the baby is like a blank slate. Brian Tracy posits that there is a theory in Psychology which says that each person comes into the world with no thoughts or ideas at all and everything that a person thinks and feels is learned from infancy onward.

The theory that the human mind is like a clean slate at birth is referred to as **TABULA RASA**. John Locke in his essay, *Concerning Human Understanding*, states the importance of human experience and concludes that the human mind at birth is a complete but receptive blank slate upon which experiences imprint on over time.

The Scottish Philosopher, David Hume supports the idea that we are born **Tabula Rasa**; a blank slate upon which the experience of the world imprints all our ideas. Over the last few decades, some philosophers and geneticists have ignored the concept of Tabula Rasa. The geneticists argue that a child's behaviour can be traced to the genetic inheritability of the child from the parents.

However, no matter the contention about the state of the mind of the child, great writers such as John Locke, David Hume, Brian Tracy, etc., believe that the adult becomes the sum total of everything he or she learns, treats and experiences, while growing up. What the adult does and becomes later is the result of early conditioning at home and the surrounding environment.

No wonder we all behave differently, the way we do. A child who leaves Africa to America at the age of seven will definitely behave more like an American when he or she is 30 years, than a child who grew up in Africa and is 30 years. The environment we live in helps to create and shape our beliefs in a very impactful way.

TABULA RASA AND FORMATION OF BELIEFS

It is an incontrovertible fact that most people have religious beliefs they inherited from their parents. There is a high probability that a child born by Hindu parents in India will practice Hinduism. A child born by Muslim parents in Saudi Arabia is most likely going to be a Muslim. More so, a child given birth to in America by a Christian family has a high tendency of being a Christian. Our parents largely influence our beliefs.

In Nigeria, we have families made up of parents who are, and whose children eventually become, doctors. In some other families, there are politicians, accountants, pastors, businessmen, etc. The role played by parents on our beliefs cannot be ignored. Our parents are our first teachers.

ENVIRONMENT AND BELIEFS

By environment, we mean our immediate location, the customs and tradition of our immediate society, the lifestyle of people living in our environment, the events and trends in our environment, the attitude of people around us, experiences in our environment, the weather and location of our environment, the type of music played in the electronic media, the level of freedom and fundamental human rights enjoyed in our area, etc.

The next time you want to do a self-introspection, ask yourself the following questions:

- What is the role of my parents in forming my beliefs from childhood?
- What impact does my environment have on my belief system?
- What other phenomena affect my belief system as I grow up?
- What impact do the books I read have on my beliefs?

☐ What impact do the people I meet every day have on my belief?

☐ What impact do religious organizations have on my belief?

☐ What impact do the things I hear every day have on my belief?

☐ What impact do the things I see every day have on my belief?

ENVIRONMENTAL FACTORS THAT LEAD TO FORMATION OF BELIEFS

RELIGIOUS/SPIRITUAL BELIEFS: People become Pagans, Christians, Muslims, Hinduists, Buddhists, etc. due to the religions practiced in their area, which they believe is true. This is difficult to change at adulthood.

FASHION AND LIFESTYLES: People wear tattoos and crazy hairdos because people around them wear such. Peer pressure affects the youth. The dressing in the western part of the world is remarkably different from the dressing in the Arab world. All these influence beliefs.

MUSIC/FILMS: The type of music we listen to also helps to form our beliefs. In some homes, parents watch films in the presence of their children; this will definitely affect the beliefs of the children when they grow up. To the children, it does not matter.

CULTURE AND TRADITION In several European countries, hard work is the order of the day. More so, in many Asian countries such as China, Japan and Indonesia, hard work is the culture in the environment, while in parts of Africa and Southern America, enjoyment and merriment are the order of the day.

GOOD GOVERNANCE AND WEALTH OF NATIONS: The mindset and beliefs of citizens in countries with great wealth, differ from those in countries where there are needs and wants. Children who were born and raised in such areas reason differently.

LEVEL OF SUPERSTITION: The more scientific a society is, the less superstitious it becomes. A lot of people, especially in the third world countries, hold superstitions in high regard, and these superstitions form a large percentage of the sum of their beliefs.

THE WEATHER AND LOCATION: The people in temperate regions tend to have more smokers of cigarette than those in the tropics. Convincing such people that smoking is wrong may be very difficult.

LEVEL OF PERSONAL LIBERTY AND FUNDAMENTAL HUMAN RIGHTS: In Countries where there is unfettered personal liberty and human rights, we hear stories of homosexuality, transgender, gender equality, rights of women, etc. While in countries where the government consider such rights as taboo, the belief of the citizens regarding such lifestyle will be almost extinct. This affects the belief of the people.

DIVERSIFIED ECONOMIES: In Countries with diversified economies, the citizens believe that money can be made through several means, including sports, entertainment, telecom, information technology, inventions, etc. In poor countries, especially third world countries, the belief in 'quick money', especially through illicit means, takes precedence over hard work.

PEOPLE WE MEET EVERYDAY: Our environment affects our belief system through the people we meet every day. If we want to be millionaires, we'll have to meet and talk with millionaires and learn their tricks. The reverse is the case when we meet negative-minded people.

The people we meet every day have an overwhelming influence in the formation of our beliefs. When we meet people that believe they can do all things, we form the belief that we too can do such. However, if we meet people that have great disbelief in themselves, we tend to lose confidence in ourselves. This eventually leads to poor performance. This explains how peer pressure destroys the youth every day.

We form our beliefs every day and some of the factors mentioned above definitely affect them. As an individual, what are the things responsible for the beliefs you have formed?

FIRST IMPRESSION MATTERS

The following first impressions may stick with us throughout lives. Brian Tracy believes that children who are raised by parents who told them how good they are, eventually grow up to become great achievers.

If parents do not know how powerful their words and advice are, they end up raising incompetent children. They produce children who believe that the world hates them and that they are less endowed. This is a major cause of failure among adults.

If a child is raised in an environment where there is no love, the child may become wicked and heartless, because of the belief that there is no love anywhere - as the Latin proverb says, *"nemo dat quod non habet"*. Meaning, you cannot give what you do not have. Such a child may become insensitive in giving and receiving human warmth because he lacks the love.

When parents call their children names such as *fool, idiot, nonentity, moron, bastard*, etc., such negative names register in them and they believe them as true and act accordingly. It will require another level of reprogramming of the mind to erase such belief from where it is stored in the subconscious mind.

As in the case of a computer, it is garbage in garbage out (GIGO). The subconscious mind is working 24 hours a day to store any information or belief the owner stores in it and it subsequently controls the behaviour of the owner.

This explains why some people have queer behaviour. These people should not be blamed; they are only acting what has been stored in their subconscious minds.

A child who grows up in a violence-prone area will not see anything wrong with violence when he or she grows up. Again, a child that is trained in a society that is ridden with drugs, prostitution, robbery, cheating, fighting and other destructive acts, may grow up to believe that these are the best ways of life. The subconscious memory registers such lifestyles in the *human hard disk* and moderates the child's behaviours to reflect what has been registered.

This explains why some teenagers smoke and drink as early as the age of thirteen or fourteen years. No matter the correction, they may believe that these are the ways of life... the best way to live.

THE AGE OF STRONG FORMATION OF BELIEF

The Psychologists of behaviour and observational learning posit that children learn through observation, imitation and modelling. Some are inclined to believe that most things parents, adults, caregivers, and even more knowledgeable others (MKO) do are true and worth emulating, even when such behaviour is an anti-social behaviour.

According to Brian Tracy, by the age of three, beliefs formed from our environment are LOCKED-IN and become fundamental part of the way children view themselves in relation to their world. Therefore, no matter what happens to them, they hold unto those beliefs in facing the reality of their existence.

WHY DO CHILDREN'S BEHAVIOURS SOMETIMES DIFFER FROM THOSE OF THEIR PARENTS?

As earlier pointed out, sometimes, parents' behaviours differ from those of their offspring. In some cases, children of pastors or clergymen behave waywardly when compared to the behaviours of their parents. The Psychologists and geneticists would tell us that some of the unwanted behaviours may come from certain latent traits in the parents' genes, which may have been transferred to the children during birth and later manifest in adulthood.

Another possible reason is that the children may have individuals outside the family whom they look up to as models, thereby conforming to these individuals' ways of life, instead of their parents. However, these are clear exceptions to the general rule. Children copy a lot as they grow, especially from the people that they live with.

Again, a child can grow up and assume a queer character due to his or her genetic make-up. Most importantly, the

role of parents and environment in the forming of beliefs of individuals cannot be overemphasized. They form the mental instructions we obey in form of beliefs.
YOUR BELIEFS ARE YOUR THOUGHTS

Your beliefs are whatever you conceive in your mind and consider to be true. Therefore, our thoughts are significant in shaping our beliefs.

Napoleon Hill posits that "if you repeat something over and over to yourself, your subconscious mind will eventually begin to accept it as fact. When something has been accepted as truth by your subconscious mind, it will work overtime to transform the idea into physical reality."

This is a case of self-fulfillment prophesy. When you repeat false reports to yourself several times a day, sooner or later, they become reality. For instance, if chicken pox invades a family, those who fear it most in the family, may become the first to contract it.

CHAPTER THREE: TYPES OF BELIEF SYSTEMS

"Your beliefs can be a prison system created by your mind for yourself. But the door is not locked. If you are aware, you are aware; you can always come out of that."

Amit Ray

There are various types of beliefs. Some of the beliefs include:

- [ ] Religious Beliefs
- [ ] Societal Beliefs
- [ ] Traditional Beliefs
- [ ] Scientific Beliefs
- [ ] Personal Beliefs
- [ ] Family Beliefs
- [ ] Superstitious Beliefs
- [ ] Fatalism

RELIGIOUS BELIEFS

These are beliefs in a Supreme Being or other gods who control the affairs of human beings on earth. Examples of religious beliefs include:

Monotheism: This is the belief in Supreme Being who created the world. Some of the religions under monotheism that are widely practiced are – Christianity, Judaism, African Traditional Religion (ATR).

Polytheism: This is the belief and worship of several gods. The word *poly* means many, and as such, several gods are worshiped under polytheism. Examples of religions that practice polytheism are Buddhism, Shintoism, Taoism, Confucianism, etc.

Theism: This is the belief in the existence of a Supreme Being or gods. Polytheism is a form of theism. With the term theism, we want to mention religions that believe in the Supreme Being.

Atheists: This group of people neither believe in the Creator, nor believe in gods. Examples of atheist groups are Agnosticism, Chinese Religion, Confucianism, Humanism, Jainism, Scientology, Shinto, Taoism.

Undefined Beliefs: Some religions that cannot be classified as part of the above religions are classified as UNDEFINED BELIEFS. Examples of such are Animism, Ancestor Worship, New Age, Shamanism, Sun Worship, Unitarian Universalism.

OTHER FORMS OF BELIEFS

People all over the world have the following forms of belief

SOCIETAL BELIEFS

These are beliefs shared by members of a given society. Usually, members of a given society identify themselves with common beliefs. Societal beliefs are akin to culture and tradition of the society. For example, some societies believe that divorce is highly unacceptable and the members frown at it vehemently.

Every society has its own beliefs which form part of the culture of the people. In some societies, it is generally believed that women are the weaker gender, and as a result, they cannot vote or drive. However, with the on-going movement of women emancipation, things are changing in their favour daily.

TRADITIONAL BELIEFS

These are beliefs which are mostly oral. They include beliefs in the Supreme Being, beliefs in spirits, beliefs in reincarnation, beliefs in Karma or retributive justice, belief in after-life, traditional medicine, etc. These traditional beliefs are handed over from generation to generation. Ethical or moral beliefs are examples of traditional beliefs. Respect for elders is a good example of traditional belief. In most African societies, children must greet the elders anytime, anywhere. Respect for parents, chiefs and leaders is more of traditional belief.

SCIENTIFIC BELIEFS

Science makes several assumptions. Scientists go ahead to prove some of these assumptions and form theories. Over the years, some of these beliefs which come in form of assumptions and theories are subsequently proven to become laws of Science.

Some known scientific laws include Drake Equation in Cosmology, Doppler Effect in Physics, Einstein's General Theory of Relativity, etc.

PERSONAL BELIEFS

Anything or something any individual holds as true is his personal belief. Personal beliefs are peculiar to individuals and emanate from religious beliefs, scientific proofs or personal experiences. Once such individual believes any of the above as true, it becomes true for the person. Personal beliefs can be described as issues or phenomena which the individual believe in as true. Personal beliefs still cover the issue of a person believing that he or she can do all things. Again, that he or she can surmount any obstacle. Once we form such belief, it becomes true.

SUPERSTITIOUS BELIEFS

Superstitious beliefs are beliefs that a group of people, society or community strongly believe in as true, without any form of proof. In the African setting, masquerades are believed to be representatives of spirits, and are therefore dreaded. Superstitious beliefs can come in form of taboos. The belief in magic is also a kind of superstitious belief... any irrational belief can be termed superstitious.

FAMILY BELIEFS

These are values and norms embedded in the families. Anything that a family holds dear and regards as true is termed 'family belief'. They can be norms and practices in the family. A man being the head of the family is a family belief and also a traditional belief. In certain families, some religious rites must be carried out before any event can occur.

FATALISM

This is the strong belief that all events and actions are already predetermined and predestined to happen. Consequently, Fatalists believe that all events in human life are inevitable. People who believe in Fatalism believe in destiny. They believe in predestination and all events of life here being preordained to happen.

CHAPTER FOUR: BELIEVE IN YOURSELF

"You cannot believe in God until you believe in yourself."

Swam Vivekanada

A strong belief in yourself is one of the most potent forces in the universe. At creation, God gave us such powers for accomplishment, if only we can believe in the God-given power within us. Most people go through life, not recognizing the unimaginable powers residing in them. Roy, T. Bennett admonishes thus: "believe in your infinite potential. Your only limitations are those you set upon yourself." Believe in yourself, your abilities and your own potentials; never let self-doubt hold you captive. In the same vein, Joy Bel declares, "the only person who can pull me down is myself, and I'm not going to let myself pull me down anymore".

Do you, out of unbelief in your God-given power, pull yourself down? Several people are down today because of lack of self-confidence, which is a psychological disorder that must be destroyed. According to Norman Vincent Peale, the greatest secret for eliminating inferiority complex, which is another term for deep and profound self-doubt, is to fill your mind, to overflowing, with faith. Develop a tremendous faith in God and that will give you a sound, realistic faith.

Again, Roy T. Bennett declares, "you should believe in yourself. You are braver than you think, more talented than you know, and more capable of more than you imagine." Do you agree with him? The truth is that at the end, men would realize that they never used up to 10 percent of their potentials and latent energy. Please, arise and change your belief. Always remember that you are permitted to start small in whatever you do, but not permitted to remain small.

REASONS FOR UNBELIEF IN ONESELF

Several reasons have been discovered to prompt people to have intense disbelief in themselves. According to Henry Miller, "what distinguishes the majority of men from the few is their ability to act according to their beliefs".

Some of these reasons are:

- Background and upbringing
- Inferiority complex
- Thought process
- Environment

BACKGROUND AND UPBRINGING

We had earlier mentioned this issue and how it affects our belief system. If we grow up in a family where our parents panic and exhibit great level of unbelief, it will definitely affect us when we become adults. When a grown individual displays behaviours close to someone not having faith, or belief in himself, then check the person's background; he must have learnt it from his or her parents. Remember, our parents are our first teachers. We copy much of their behaviours, whether good or bad, including lack of belief in oneself. Above all, some parents cage their children till they become adults, thus all that the children know must have been imbibed from their parents. According to G-Dragon, "you have to believe in yourself, challenge yourself and push yourself, until the even end, that's the only way you will succeed."

INFERIORITY COMPLEX

When we feel that other people are better than us and rationalize this thought, then we exhibit inferiority complex. This psychological disorder has affected and prevented many men and women from reaching their life goals and endeavours. With inferiority complex, we sell ourselves short. If we cannot believe in ourselves, we do not have any reason to ask other people to believe in us.

THOUGHT PROCESS

We think of too many things in one second. The average human mind is very active. It analyzes events and issues pictorially. Our minds are like a garden and if properly cultivated, it will produce good fruits, but if not properly maintained, it will grow weed.

According to Norman Vincent Pearl, "we build up the feeling of insecurity or security by how we think. If in our thoughts, we constantly fix attention upon sinister expectations of dire events that might happen, the result will be to constantly feel insecure". What is even more serious is the tendency to create, by the power of thought, the very condition we fear. We must monitor what we think. If we believe that God has given us tremendous power to excel in life, it automatically becomes our reality, and by the law of attraction, we attract such things we think about. The caution here is, 'be careful of what you think; it may become your reality'. This is a piece of advice from Brian Tracy. According to him, the way you think and feel about yourself, including your beliefs and expectations about what is possible for you, determines everything you do and everything that happens to you. When you change the quality of your thinking, you change the quality of your life, sometimes instantly.

ENVIRONMENT

Here, the environment covers the people around us, the society we live in, our cultures and traditions. These factors in our environment can create strong lack of self-belief. In an environment that high level of superstition is the order of the day, most people easily give up on life, believing that no matter what they do, it would not amount to anything. Over the years, such thinking seeps inside the subconscious mind of the individuals who believe that they were created to suffer on earth.

Environment has made several people who were created to be billionaires, to live just as paupers. This is unfair. David J. Schwartz in his book titled, *The Magic of Thinking Big,* advices us to – *"believe it can be done. When you believe something can be done (really believe), your mind will find the ways to do it. Believing a solution, paves the way to a solution."*

PROBING QUESTIONS

- Do you believe that you were created to be a victor and not a victim?
- Do you have fears over your abilities?
- Do you think other people are better than you?
- Do you have feelings that your upbringing has affected you the way you see things?
- Do you believe that your mind is always skewed towards things that discourage you?
- Do you always see dangers instead of solutions?

GOOD NEWS

Sit down and relax. By the time you finish reading this book, all your fears will disappear, and you will re-engineer yourself mentally and spiritually for great success. Enough is enough! This is the time to change your frequency in belief. Believe in yourself!

STEPS TO BELIEVING IN YOURSELF

1. Mentally assess where you are right now. Are you satisfied?
2. Mentally picture where you should be and your level of achievements and your heart desires. Write down your heart desires and goals for the next one year.
3. Commit them to God in prayers, morning, and night, before you sleep.
4. What are the possible challenges that may affect your ability to accomplish these goals? Write them down.
5. Commit the challenges to God Almighty in prayers, daily.
6. Face the challenges and tackle them one after the other.
7. Pray, morning and night, committing yourself to God, and asking for divine power and guidance to conquer the obstacles.
8. Make detailed plans to achieve your goals.
9. Take actions. Meet the people that will assist you to achieve the goals. Invest your resources.
10. Keep believing that it is possible.

11. Give thanks and celebrate any achievement, no matter how little, and keep praying against negative thoughts and thoughts of unbelief.

12. Please, urgently remember what Brad Henry said. According to him, *"believe in yourself, and the rest will fall in place. Have faith in your own abilities, work hard and there is nothing you cannot accomplish."*

CHAPTER FIVE: BELIEVE IN GOD ALMIGHTY

"Let your life reflect the faith you have in God. Fear nothing and pray about everything. Be strong, trust God's word and trust the process."

Germany Kent

Belief in God Almighty is the panacea for all human problems. It is called faith, and it is the most potent source of energy or force in our known universe. The creator of the universe is God Almighty.

Joel Osteen once said, *"resist discouragement by speaking his word over your future. Keep standing, keep hoping and keep believing, because he is working behind the scenes. He is going to accelerate your times and lead you into the life of victory he has for you."* Also, Hendrith Smith states, *"we are composed of the same energy and quanta of that which composes everything. We are co-composers of the universe, thinkers of the only mind that thinks, co-creators with the God that is creating us".*

Scientists are of the view that apart from our galaxy which harbours our star called the sun; Hubble Telescope reveals that there are over 100 billion galaxies occupying the space out there. The belief that the universe has a beginning and it is expanding like an inflated balloon shows that at a time, there was no universe until the Great

Creator caused things to happen. Some scientists called this *The Big Bang*, which they estimated took place about 13.7 billion years ago.

The sun is about 93 million miles from our Earth, yet we feel its scotching impact in the equator heat. It is estimated that the energy generated in a second by the nuclear fusion of hydrogen gas in the sun if deployed on earth is capable of giving electricity to all households for 365 days. God is Mighty!

THE UNIVERSE IN NUMBERS

Scientists have estimated the following:
- There are over 7 quintillion grains of sand on world's beaches.
- There are over 1 septillion of stars in the universe.
- There are about 920 to 3,170 octillion microbes in the planet.
- The Earth's interior may be filled with a quadrillion tone of diamonds.
- There are about 3 trillion trees in the world (www.live science.com).
- An average male produces around 525 billion sperm cells over a lifetime and loses around millions of them a month.
- Women are born with 2 million egg follicles, but only about 450 eggs mature for fertilization in their lifetime.

- An average human being has over 100 billion neurons in his brain that interact with each other every second.
- There are 1 billion planets, which orbit a super massive black hole (space.com).
- There are over 500,000 pieces of space junk, both meteors and artificial particles, larger than the size of a marble, that orbit the earth; yet earth is protected from their impact in case most of them fall off and hit the earth.

No wonder David proclaimed in Psalm 8:3-6, *"when I consider your Heavens, the work of your fingers, the moon and the stars which you have set in place, what is mankind that you are mindful of them; human beings that you care for them? You have made them a little lower than the angels and crowned them with glory and honour. You made them rulers over the works of your hands. You put everything under their feet".*

From the above we need to understand that God Almighty is great. We must believe in God who meets the needs of all living things. Psalms: 14:16 says, *"thou openest thine hand and satisfies the desire of every living thing".*

HOW TO TAP INTO THE ENERGY OF THE UNIVERSE THROUGH PRAYER

We must pray without ceasing; prayer is powerful. Norman Vincent Pearl has this to say about prayer –

"people are doing more praying than ever before, because they find that it adds to personal efficiency."

Prayer helps them to tap into forces and to utilize strength not otherwise available. A famous psychologist said, *"prayer is the greatest power available to the individual in solving his problems. Prayer power is manifestation of energy"*. Just as there exists scientific techniques for the release of atomic energy, so are there scientific procedures for the release of spiritual energy through the mechanism of prayer. The exciting demonstration of this energizing force is evidently what prayer does for you.

WHAT IS A PRAYER?

Prayer is a solemn request or expression of thanks addressed to God. For Pastor Billy Graham, prayer is *"spiritual communication between man and God; a two-way relationship in which man should not only talk to God but also listen to him"*. Prayer to God is like a child's conversation with his father. For Charles Spurgeon, true prayer is neither a mere mental exercise nor a vocal performance. It is far deeper than that; it is spiritual transaction with the creator of Heaven and Earth.

In the first book on this series "The Prayers That Run" (*TPTR*), Prayer was defined as what you do to complete your second-to-second life cycle. You pray to keep your life connected to the owner; to keep the root of your life nourished from its source. You must pray because the life you live is not yours; to keep living, you must continuously present yourself to be watered by your designer. The book in an eye opening and soul piercing manner, also described prayer as what you need to do if you want to continue to remain connected to the source of your life -- God, NOT what you do when you are in need.

Joyce Meyer said prayer is simply talking to God like a friend and should be the easiest thing we do each day. Norman Vincent Pearle posits – *"personally, I believe that prayer is a send-out of vibrations from one person to another, and to God. All of the universe is in vibration. There are vibrations in the molecules of a table. The air is filled with vibrations. The reaction between human beings is also a vibration. When you send out a prayer for another person, you employ the force inherent in a spiritual universe. You transport from yourself to the other person, sense of love, helpfulness, support, powerful understanding, and in this process, you awaken vibration in the universe, through which God brings to pass the good objectives prayed for"*.

From the above, we can deduce the following:
- The power of prayer seems able to normalize the aging process.
- Prayer obviates and limits infirmity and deterioration.
- Prayer can freshen you up every evening, and send you out renewed, each morning.
- You can receive guidance in problems if prayer is allowed to permeate your subconscious.

- ☐ Prayer has the power to keep your reactions correct and sound.
- ☐ Prayer driven deeply into the subconscious can remake you.
- ☐ Prayer releases and keeps power flowing freely.

ABSOLUTE BELIEF IN GOD

For us to conquer the world's challenges, we must urgently go back to God, and learn new techniques of pragmatic prayers. Paul, in Philippians 4:6 writes, *"do not fret or have any anxiety about anything, but in every circumstance and everything by prayer and petitions with thanksgiving, continue to make your wants known to God."* The belief in God's power in our affair is not negotiable; it should form part of our belief system.

BELIEVE IN THE GOD OF ABUNDANCE

You must believe in the God who provides everything in great abundance, as stated in Psalm 50:10-12 – *"for every beast of the forest is mine and the cattle upon a thousand hills or upon the mountains where thousands are. I know the birds of the mountains and the wild animals of the field are mine and are with me in mind."*

Psalm 24:1 says, *"the Earth is the Lord's and the fullness of it; the world and they who dwell in it."*

When God created the universe and our dear Earth, He did not manage resources. Believe in God Almighty and you will see things in your reality changing according to your belief. Remember, *believing is seeing,* not *seeing is believing.* Mahatma Gandhi declared: *"but for my faith in God, I should have been a raving maniac".*

THE EARTH IN NUMBERS

Some useful facts describe the power of the Almighty:
- The Earth's orbital speed around the sun is 30km/second or 1,000km/hour... yet we do not fall off.
- The sun's orbital speed around the galaxy is 200km/second, and about 720,000km/hour.
- The Earth is about 93 million miles from the sun.
- The Earth is programmed to move at about 66,000 miles per hour through space to complete its 365 days a year rotation.
- The earth's atmosphere is 78% nitrogen, 21% oxygen and 1% other ingredients.
- Only the earth has a breathable atmosphere.
- The earth has a diameter of about 8000 miles (13,000 kilometres).
- Water covers over 70% of the Earth's surface.
- It takes Earth 23.934 hours to complete a rotation of its axis.

- [ ] It takes the Earth 365.26 days to complete an orbit round the sun.
- [ ] Our Earth is a bit closer to the sun in early January and farther away in July.
- [ ] Air surrounds Earth and becomes thinner farther from the surface; roughly 100 miles (160km) above the Earth, the air becomes so thin.

If God could keep the delicate balance in nature, so as to sustain life on Earth, won't he do much more with humans? We were created to serve and worship Him. Let us develop unshakeable belief in God.

CHAPTER SIX: WHAT IS FALSE BELIEF?

"Your Belief system consists of the power to create and to destroy."

Tobi Delly

There are two major classes of beliefs. They are:

- ☐ Non-beneficial belief or false belief
- ☐ Beneficial beliefs (these beliefs will be treated in chapter seven.

NON-BENEFICIAL BELIEFS OR FALSE BELIEFS

These are those beliefs, concepts, perspectives, definitions, phenomena that we have accepted as true, but are actually false. That is, in actual sense, they are not true. For instance, a child having fever should not eat groundnut (peanut) or oily foods, as such would exacerbate the illness. Superstitions come under false beliefs.

COUNTERFEIT BELIEFS

What are counterfeit beliefs? As the name implies, these are fake beliefs. They are not original or genuine. These are beliefs which we believe are true, but they contradict the truth. These are beliefs that are not real, but we accept them as true.

Raisedfrequency.com, an internet-based publishing outfit has this to say about counterfeit belief – *"the explanation of why counterfeit beliefs are deceiving can be found in the way the* **Law of Attraction** *works. When we believe something to be true, we are broadcasting the frequency of that truth and the holographic universe brings opportunities and people that are a match to our truth, then it is physically manifested"*.

Examples of counterfeit beliefs are:

- ☐ The belief that you can make money without working hard.
- ☐ The belief that most rich people became rich through luck, when they actually worked for money, before they became rich.
- ☐ Another clear example is the exhibition of inferiority complex; the belief that other people are better than us. The grass looks greener in another person's compound.

WHAT ARE SELF LIMITING BELIEFS?

Self-limiting beliefs are a set of beliefs that hold us down, limit our potentials and keep us in a self-imposed prison of lack of confidence, lack of belief in our ability, feeling of unproductiveness and inappropriate attitude towards life's struggles. These beliefs are programmed in our subconscious mind and manipulate us to live below our capacities, accepting that we are victims, not victors of the game of life.

The acceptance of self-limiting beliefs always inhibits the success story of the individuals. These beliefs make us see only the dark side of life. When an individual believes that life is a struggle, truly, he interprets all events of life as struggle. This has rendered many people's lives, hell on earth.

EXAMPLES OF SELF-LIMITING BELIEFS

- Other people are luckier than I am.
- Why me?
- Why do I have several enemies?
- Other people are more brilliant than I am.
- What have I done to people that they hate me?
- People are responsible for everything that happens to me.
- I am not good enough.
- I am not handsome or beautiful.
- Other persons progress because people love them more than me.
- I am not able to do it.
- You know I cannot talk fast.
- My parents did not train me well.

- ☐ My parents did not leave resources for me.
- ☐ My body is too slim/fat.
- ☐ All fingers are not equal.
- ☐ I cannot cope with the rush.
- ☐ I am trying my best, but things are not working out the way I want them to.
- ☐ This is a hopeless situation.
- ☐ I give up.
- ☐ I am not capable of achieving any thing in life.
- ☐ My small salary cannot do anything for me.
- ☐ Wealthy People are wicked.
- ☐ I am not loveable.
- ☐ I am too fragile.
- ☐ My people always abandon me.
- ☐ My Organization is wicked.
- ☐ I cannot achieve anything without my salary.
- ☐ To be successful, I have to pretend to be someone that I am not.

OTHER FORMS OF SELF-LIMITING BELIEFS

These self -limiting Beliefs can sometimes come in the form of IF NOT.

- ☐ If not for my bad voice, I would have been a singer.
- ☐ If not for my parents, I would have achieved much.
- ☐ If not for my relations who hate me, I would have made it.
- ☐ If not for my poor educational background, I would have been successful.

- [ ] If not that I am so dark, people would have loved me.
- [ ] If not that I am from this part of the country, I would have gotten a better job.
- [ ] If not that I am black, I would have travelled abroad.
- [ ] If not that I am not intelligent enough, I would have passed all my courses.
- [ ] If not that I cannot speak other languages, I would have made it.
- [ ] If not that I am short, I would have excelled.
- [ ] If not for my parents, I would have been celebrated.
- [ ] If not that jobs are scarce in the country, I would have been working long ago.
- [ ] If not that there isn't enough time, I would be ahead of others.

We need to know that IF NOTS are forms of self-limiting beliefs. These self-limiting beliefs hold us to the ground for several years. This is the time to say enough is enough.

WHAT ARE DISEMPOWERING BELIEFS

Self-disempowering beliefs are beliefs which portray us as *powerless*. They are weakening... they are incapacitating. Any individual who sees himself or herself as a victim of life, is most likely enslaved by disempowering beliefs. Once an individual believes he or she cannot do anything tangible, the forces in the universe will make it to come to pass. These beliefs drain your powers. There is a popular saying that *"if you think you can or cannot, you are right"*. Disempowering beliefs rob us of the beauty of life. They make life hellish.

Examples of disempowering beliefs are:
- People get what they do not deserve.
- I cannot read for long.
- Please don't rush me.
- I get tired easily.
- It is too difficult for me to handle.
- I am not destined to achieve this level of success.
- People take advantage of me.
- Rich people go to hell.
- Being poor is a virtue.
- There is no time for anything.

According to Raisefrequency.com, if you believe you are powerless, the universe will mirror back to you scenarios and people that will make you feel like a victim of life. The *Law of Attraction* reinforces what you believe and accept as true without any opinion or judgment of it. Your subconscious mind then makes you look at life as unpleasant. You see life as monotonous and unfair; you feel neglected by everybody and look at people with suspicion. On the contrary, a young businessman who does his health status checks every month told his doctor: *"life is sweet, but don't tell anybody."*

CHAPTER SEVEN: WHAT ARE BENEFICIAL BELIEFS?

"Believe that life is worth living and your belief will help create the fact."

Williams James

As the name implies, beneficial beliefs are beliefs that are useful, rewarding and generate good results for the believer. Beneficial beliefs are life enhancing beliefs that tend to be uplifting, and over the years, enable the person or the believer to see the good side of life, and to a large extent, be successful in several spheres of human endeavours. Beneficial beliefs enable the believer to live a fulfilling life. William James says that pessimism leads to weakness; optimism leads to power.

Examples of beneficial beliefs are:

- God created me for a purpose.
- I am a likeable person.
- I am created in the image of God Almighty.
- Life is good; life is sweet.
- I am here to conquer.
- I am destined for success.
- I am stable in all things.
- I have all it takes to be successful.

- ☐ I can do all things through Christ who strengthens me.
- ☐ I came, I saw, I conquered.
- ☐ There are enough resources for everyone on earth.
- ☐ God gives me strength to make wealth according to Deut. 8:18.
- ☐ I can achieve my goals in life easily.
- ☐ Being rich is my destiny.
- ☐ I choose to be happy.
- ☐ I am fearfully and wonderfully made.
- ☐ Success locates me easily.
- ☐ Life is fun.
- ☐ I must invest in myself.
- ☐ Everything is possible to anyone that believes.
- ☐ I am worthy to be alive.
- ☐ I am unstoppable
- ☐ The world is at my feet.

A LOOK AT THE DIFFERENCES BETWEEN BENEFICIAL AND NON-BENEFICIAL BELIEFS

S/N	Non-Beneficial Beliefs	Beneficial Beliefs
1	The universe is not supporting anyone.	The universe supports me 24 hours a day.
2	I am looking for success.	Success finds me everywhere I go.

3	It is not easy to make a comfortable living in this part of the country.	Comfortable living is my birthright.
4	It is difficult to make it in this country.	It is very easy to make it in this country.
5	People don't like me.	People like me everywhere I go.
6	Happiness is elusive.	Happiness is my choice.
7	What a hopeless country.	I have hope that I will make it in this country.
8	If only my health was good enough...	My health is good enough. Isaiah 53:5
9	If only I was educated, I would have achieved a great deal.	Even without enough education, I can make it.
10	If only someone would help me...	I look up to God for my help.
11	Making money is difficult.	Making money is easy and sweet if I know the process.
12	This world is hazardous.	This world is safe, my GOD is in charge. Ps. 91:1-2

13	Life is not easy.	Life is easy.
14	Being poor is a virtue.	Being poor is never a virtue; I must be rich.
15	I must cheat to make it.	I don't have to cheat to make it.
16	You must know someone before you get a job.	I don't need to know someone to get a job.

CHAPTER EIGHT: DANGEROUS EXPRESSIONS THAT INCAPACITATE YOU

"Nobody can motivate himself in a positive direction by continually using negative words."

John C. Maxwell

Some dangerous expressions that destroy our abilities and encourage disbeliefs include:

- I cannot!
- I do not deserve it.
- I am unworthy.
- I am disadvantaged.
- Life is full of risks.

Let us discuss each of these core beliefs or dangerous expressions briefly.

I CANNOT DO IT

Children grow up to discover to their chagrin that their parents and immediate environment have programmed their subconscious mind to declare that they cannot shoulder certain responsibilities, even without making any attempt in the first place. According to an online publisher, *"unfortunately, most children are taught a long list of **you can't** and **we can't**, early in life. Therefore, most of us are short-circuited from a large position of our potentials."*

The failure in adult life can be traced to series of *I can't,* which parents transferred to their children. Granted that most parents are ill-educated and not exposed, they in turn mold their children in their limited views of life, thereby indirectly enforcing the vicious level of poverty from generation to generation.

"Don't do this! Don't do that! You cannot achieve this! You were not born with a silver spoon in life so maintain your class." All these expressions are programmed in a child's subconscious mind, thereby limiting the child's success level in life, later on.

Norman Vincent Peale articulated this truism in his book, *You Can If You Think You Can.* When you think you can, then you can achieve it. For Henry Ford, *"whether you think you can, or you think you can't, you are right".*

Wonderlustworker.com writes and supports Henry Ford this way – *"one of the fabled sayings that resonate most with me comes from Henry Ford. He says, "if you think you can or you cannot, you are right'. To me, it speaks volumes. Most of us fail before we even start to work towards a goal, because we lack belief in ourselves. If you don't believe you can achieve something, how can you expect to follow through with it or expect other people to believe in you?"*

If you don't believe in yourself, you cannot convince other people to believe in you. To buttress the importance of belief, William James, stated emphatically, *"it is our attitude at the beginning of a difficult task which, more than anything else, will affect its successful outcome."* Here, he refers to attitude as belief in yourself. Again, he expressed eloquently, *"believe that life is worth living and your belief will help create the fact"*.

I DO NOT DESERVE IT

Some individuals grow up with so much self-doubt, due to the conditioning by their parents, who programmed them to believe that they do not deserve riches, fame, education, good health, financial resources, properties, etc. Due to the limited knowledge of how the universe runs, most parents teach their children to believe that people with great wealth have already been destined to be wealthy and there is nothing they can do about it. Mind you, some of these parents have limited exposures. To cap it all, children of such parents grow up believing that all the resources in the world belong to certain class of people. In some societies, we have the caste system which sidelines some people as destined to be slaves to others.

Any child who grows up in such environment believes that he or she does not deserve to be wealthy. This belief is a bad one as it destroys the potentials of such individuals and makes them victims of life. This is one of the self-limiting beliefs that destroy destinies over the centuries.

If you are reading this book and you have ever contemplated such thought, flush it out. It is an evil thought that can torment one for life and be passed on to the next generation.

I AM UNWORTHY

Some adults have grown up to the point where they feel they are unworthy to manage any position. They have serious self-doubt. Such individuals believe that they are disadvantaged by virtue of unknown factors or family background. Psychologists believe that people suffering from this inferiority malady actually need counselling in order to make them more assertive.

By creation, we are all worthy to enjoy God's goodies on Earth. We are worthy to enjoy the sunshine, the cool weather, the moon, healthy living and other beauties of nature. Over the years, our culture, society and our environments make us believe falsely that we are unworthy to receive good things. Remember, you are worthy to enjoy the riches of the world. God Almighty is your creator and Father.

I AM DISADVANTAGED

Some parents erroneously tell their children that they are not qualified to make it in life, while some others teach their children that only the rich men's children get good jobs. This explains why some people use bleaching cream to remove the black pigmentation of their skin; because they believe that fair is good, while being dark is a big disadvantage. Naomi Campbell is dark, yet she is an international model. People all over the world who do not believe they are disadvantaged keep doing well. Please, dear reader, do not believe that you have any disadvantage whatever. Do not believe that life is not fair. Believe that life is fair to all. Sometimes in life, students who scored 'A$_s$' in examinations, end up working for students who scored 'C$_s$'.

LIFE IS FULL OF RISKS

Some parents put fear into their children. They teach them that life is full of risks. Their children grow up to believe this statement, which is false. With this belief solidly laid in their subconscious, these children grow up as adults, avoiding risks. To them, everything is risky. To some people, there is no need to take certain jobs because of the inherent risks. The fear of risk has left certain individuals unfulfilled and unable to achieve their goals in life. They get old without achieving much. At this point, the issue of vicious cycle of poverty comes to mind; the fear of risk now renders almost a whole generation unproductive.

CHAPTER NINE: BELIEVING IS SEEING, NOT SEEING IS BELIEVING

"Faith is taking the first step, even when you don't see the whole staircase."

Martin Luther King Jnr.

Most people express the popular dictum, *seeing is believing!* However, I consider the reverse as the case. When we believe, then we see it happening. The fact is that when we believe in something, we interpret events and circumstances in line with what we already believed in, which then becomes our reality. By the *Law of Expectation*, we experience self-fulfilling prophecies: for you to achieve success in life, you must first believe, and by the Law of Expectation, the belief becomes your reality.

It is therefore safe to say that we believe and experience what we already believed in. If a student believes that a subject or course is difficult, automatically, by Law of Expectation, he is likely to fail the test and will justify himself by concluding, *"I said it; I knew that I would not pass the exam"*. The student forgets that he had failed the examination even before sitting for it.

For the reader, believe you will succeed, and the universe will work in your favour to succeed.

UNIVERSAL LAWS THAT ACTIVATE BELIEFS IN OUR LIVES

After the universe was created by the Great Creator and owner of the universe, some laws were put in place to guide existence. Some of these laws are physical, while others are metaphysical. When all the planets revolve round their stars, they are only obeying a law. There cannot be a law without a law giver; there cannot be a programme without a programmer.

We are told that there are several other solar systems, with planets and suns around which these planets revolve. This is called *Multilevel Universe*. On planet Earth, there are unwritten laws that govern existence, which make beliefs very powerful and affect our lives positively or negatively. Some of the laws are:

Law of Belief: This means that whatever assumption we believe as true, becomes our reality. If an individual believes that he will be ill, it will not be too long before he becomes ill. The person attracts it into his other life. The body cells become weak and obey the instructions to be ill. The subconscious mind takes command from you and acts accordingly.

Law of Expectation: This law explains that whatever we expect becomes our reality. If you expect to be successful in a venture, it would not be long before the results become reality. Here, we call it self-fulfilling prophesy.

Law of Attraction: This law states that whatever we focus on, day and night, will eventually be attracted to us. Anything we pray for and concentrate on, will make us attract people, circumstances and resources that will make such thoughts become reality in our lives.

Law of Polarity: This law states that the world is divided into two parts, and for every good thing, there must be a corresponding negative version. Examples are: good and bad, black and white, sun and moon, big and small, male and female, etc. We have positive and negative vibrations. If you focus or believe in the negative it becomes a reality and vice versa.

Law of Correspondence: This law states that what is impressed is expressed and that the outside of a person reflects what is inside. A frowning face is a reflection of internal bitterness.

Law of Cause and Effect: The law says that whatever action we take will lead to effects. For every cause or event, there must be a corresponding effect.

Law of Accumulation: The law says that the daily actions or activities we undertake, end up accumulating into big achievement, just like little drops of water.

Law of Habit: When a new habit takes the place of old habit, we say the Law of Habit is at work. Anything we do repeatedly becomes new habit.

Law of Action: The law says that when we take action concerning what we want, we inch towards achieving our goal. Action takes us closer to our target. If we want anything, we must take action. Lack of action keeps us on the same sport year in, year out.

CHAPTER TEN: BELIEFS AFFECT YOUR LIFE

"It is what you choose to believe that makes you the person you are."

Karen Marie Moning

Feelings of hopelessness and helplessness over issues of life are all effects of our belief.

Negative Belief/Limiting Belief: There is nothing anyone can do to change the situation. People accept circumstances in their lives as things already ordained or programmed to take place. This is a form of belief called *fatalism*. Some parents implant in their children, the negative belief that wealth is meant for certain categories of people. The children grow up believing that they can do little or nothing to change the circumstances they are facing.

Positive Belief: There is something someone can do for every situation. Positive belief teaches us that we are not helpless. We are unstoppable. We can decree a thing and it shall come to pass. Religious faith teaches us that if life gives us a lemon, we can make lemonade. More so, positive belief teaches us that no situation is permanent. It is not a hopeless situation. It shall always come to pass.

Decision: This is the type of belief which considers that God has given you power to crush and decimate all challenges of life. By the *Law of Expectations* and the *Law of Action*, you will come out victorious. So, never believe that a situation is hopeless because you have been given the power to surmount all obstacles. If your parents or environment implanted this self-limiting belief, quietly analyze the situation, and expunge it from where it was impressed on your subconscious mind. Take appropriate actions to reverse the inimical situation. Liberate yourself with a new level of thought. Think positively to destroy the negative belief.

BELIEF AND HEALTH ISSUES – HOW BELIEFS AFFECT YOUR HEALTH

Negative Belief (Limiting Belief): A small injury on the body can become a major health concern if the individual believes that such injury was caused by his or her enemies. Negative beliefs bring all manners of illnesses, such as high blood pressure, ulcers, insomnia, heart issues, weakness of the bone, constipation, and sundry illnesses. When individuals entertain negative beliefs such as – they were created with health defects, they are not supposed to have good health, all illnesses are sent by the enemies, etc., the ill conditions are aggravated. By the *Law of Attraction*, such individuals attract more illnesses into their bodies. The subconscious mind ensures that sicknesses become the order of the day of a warped mindset. Negative beliefs make injuries to not heal fast, because the body system is in a dysfunctional state.

POSITIVE BELIEF

Positive thoughts have healing effects. The Bible says, *"a merry heart does good like medicine"*. When an individual has positive beliefs, the body parts receive positive information from the mind, and illness will be chased very far. Christians always believe that by the stripes of Jesus they are healed.

Strong positive belief in the God of healing has therapeutic effect on the body. A recent report titled, *"Going To Church Could Help You Live Longer"*, anchored by Carina Storrs on CNN, on May 16, 2016, showed that many Americans say that they attend church because it helps them stay grounded and gives them spiritual guidance. The study also however suggested that regular attendance may also help increase their life span.

During a research that involved about 75,000 middle-age female nurses in the United States, as part of the Nurses' Health Study, the Participants answered questions on whether they attend religious services regularly every four years, between 1992 and 2012, and about other aspects of their lives over the years. Amazingly, the researcher found out that women who went to church more than once a week had a 33% lower risk of dying during the study period, compared with those who said that they never went. Women who attended church once a week or less, had 26% and 13% lower risk of death, respectively. The report concludes that going to church could have a number of additional benefits that could in turn improve longevity.

DECISION

Believe that you are healthy, and that God can give good health and you will attract it into your life based on absolute faith in God. For good health, you must have life enhancing beliefs. Belief in God will make your body to be in a functional state instead of dysfunctional state.

IMPACT OF BELIEF ON FEAR

Positive belief dismantles and utterly liquidates all elements of fear. Psychological disorders sometimes result from self-limiting belief. Wikipedia views fear as a feeling induced by perceived danger or threat that occurs in certain types of organisms, which causes a change in metabolic and organic functions, and ultimately, a change in behaviour such as feeling, including freezing from perceived traumatic events.

Remember: The mind is so powerful in twisting issues and events and viewing things from negative position.

NEGATIVE BELIEF OR LIMITING BELIEF

Expressions of SELF-LIMITING BELIEFS concerning fear include:

- ☐ I fear for my life.
- ☐ I fear that I may not pass the exam.
- ☐ I am afraid that our vehicle may break down.
- ☐ I am scared of large audiences.
- ☐ I am scared of Mathematics.
- ☐ I am scared of talking in public.
- ☐ I fear walking in the night.

Some people fear cockroaches, mice, goats, etc. Many people live in morbid fear, throughout their lives. Over 50% of people living in this world live in fear. However, we should know that God has not given us spirit of fear, but of power and of love and of sound mind; so says the Bible in 2 Timothy 1:7. The holy books of other religions also believe that man should not fear. Even in the Bible, God empowered man to dominate the world. Despite religious teachings in Islam, Christianity, Buddhism, etc. man still exhibits the following types of fears.

TYPES OF FEARS (IRRATIONAL FEARS)

- ☐ Trypophobia - The fear of holes.
- ☐ Aerophobia - The fear of flying.
- ☐ Mysophobia - The fear of germs.
- ☐ Claustrophobia - The fear of small spaces.
- ☐ Astraphobia - The fear of thunder and lightning.
- ☐ Cynophobia - The fear of dogs.

- ☐ Agoraphobia - The fear of open or crowded spaces.
- ☐ Acrophobia - The fear of heights.
- ☐ Ophidiophobia - The fear of snakes.
- ☐ Arachnophobia - The fear of spiders.

Other Basic Fears of Man Include:
- ☐ The fear of poverty.
- ☐ The fear of criticism.
- ☐ The fear of ill health.
- ☐ The fear of death.
- ☐ The fear of not finding love.
- ☐ The fear of old age.

Which of these fears do you harbour? Please discard them. They are dangerous to your health, and especially to your existence.

It can be concluded that fear and anxiety have several unpleasant consequences, most especially on health. Negative beliefs or self-limiting beliefs give rise to fear, and constant morbid fear has the following dangerous consequences:

Fear weakens our immune system and can cause cardio-muscular damages, gastrointestinal problems such as ulcers, irritable bowel syndrome and decreased fertility. It can lead to accelerated aging and even premature death.

Fear can damage the formation of long-term memories and causes serious damages to some parts of the brain. Fear can create psychosomatic sickness, which actually does not exist. The world becomes a fearful place.

Fear affects and distorts processes in our brains which naturally assist us to regulate and manage our emotions, our thinking and decision making. Fear leads to clinical depression.

By the *Law of Attraction*, people attract those things they openly or secretly fear, into their lives. Please, if you meet Job in the Bible, ask him; all he feared befell him. By the *Law of Correspondence,* the fear an individual harbours, reflects in the victim's lifestyle and character, and that explains why some people cannot have smiles on their faces throughout the year; simply because of the unstoppable fear that they harbour daily. This must stop for individuals to enjoy life and enjoy it more abundantly. Change your beliefs and change your life immediately.

POSITIVE BELIEFS

To live a fruitful and productive life, an individual must conquer the emotion of fear. Fear is a destroyer of destiny. It is destructive; it kills. People who fear are less efficient.

To be victorious in life, one must abolish fear. The absence of fear is faith. The following expressions of affirmations help to abolish fear:

- God has not given us a spirit of fear, but of a sound mind.
- Fear will be afraid of me.
- I am a child of God; I shall not fear.

- ☐ My protection is in God's hands; why shall I fear?
- ☐ The Lord is my light and my salvation, whom shall I fear or dread? The Lord is the refuge and stronghold of my life, of whom shall I be afraid? Psalms 27:1.
- ☐ I shall live in victory.
- ☐ The Lord God is a strong tower; the righteous shall run into it and they are saved.

Before we conclude this aspect of fear with the decision we should make, it would be highly apposite to look at the feature of fear generally:

- ☐ Fear gives life to lifeless issues.
- ☐ Fear makes a case look hopeless even when there are signs that things could get better.
- ☐ Fear robs you of your joy.
- ☐ Fear makes a case more intricate or seemingly complex to solve. It makes a small problem look big.
- ☐ Fear creates a new problem which must be solved before you solve the main problem (dire circumstances which are not part of the original).
- ☐ Fear incapacitates its victim.
- ☐ Fear denies its victims rational reasons.
- ☐ Fear creates panic and tension.
- ☐ Fear makes people susceptible to scam and fraud.
- ☐ Fear makes everything look dangerous and unreliable.
- ☐ Fear makes people desperate.

HOW YOUR BELIEF AFFECTS YOUR BEHAVIOUR

When people say a person has a queer character, it means that the person is acting out his belief, which the average man views as outrageous or out rightly abnormal. It is called *strange behaviour*. Some behavioural patterns are repulsive because the persons involved, harbour strange beliefs, which they have programmed into their subconscious mind and move around with them. They do not care how other people feel about them. They are like mobile bombs waiting to detonate on anyone they meet.

An internet-based publishing outfit, Toknowmyself.com, mentions the various ways that belief affects behaviour. They are:

Belief and self-confidence: People that have self-confidence have actually developed powerful beliefs over the years, thereby making them immune to fear. Self-limiting beliefs make people to shy away from their goals. People who have such beliefs easily conclude that other people are better than them. They sell themselves below their value, they avoid people, they cannot talk in public, they are easily hurt by people's expressions, they prefer to stay alone, they are very antagonistic and resentful, and they take offence at little jokes.

Beliefs and Information filtering: We filter information in our minds based on our beliefs, and only absorb the information that matches our beliefs. This is why persuading someone to change his or her religious beliefs is very difficult. If a Hindu adherent wants to convert a Christian or vice versa, it would be very difficult. Although we have exceptions, when people get converted easily, 98% of the time, it is difficult to change the information about beliefs already embedded in a person's subconscious, which manipulate the person on daily basis. The reason is because, as individuals grow up, their subconscious minds get configured to accept that their beliefs are the best.

Belief and Crimes: People who commit crimes do so because of their beliefs. Some people commit vices because they believe that the society has abandoned them, while others exhibit anti-social behaviours because they believe that wealth is unequally distributed. To make matters worse, some children grow with the belief that taking what does not belong to them is normal. They grow up seeing their parents collect other people's properties without qualms, and they accept this as the best way of life. Crimes committed all over the world stem from the fact that people believe that there isn't anything wrong with committing such crimes, so they (the criminals) justify such crimes. Right from the time of Adam and Eve, mankind has not changed. The average man does not accept blame.

In his book, *How to Win Friends and Influence People,* Dale Carnegie narrated the gory detail of how a criminal called 'Two-gun Crowley', who killed a cop, declared that he was arrested because he was defending himself. He never accepted that he was a die-hard criminal, who killed cops. Why did the *cop-killer* behave that way? The reason is simple. He believed that there was nothing wrong with stealing or killing. He believed that shooting a cop is a form of self-defense. Too bad!

It is safe to conclude that beliefs make people commit crimes and justify their actions. This makes an interesting topic in psychology and will assist to get rid of our society of crime. People commit crime principally because of their warped belief that crime pays. We can change lives by changing people's beliefs. This is why we have rehabilitation homes.

EFFECT OF BELIEF ON ACHIEVEMENT AND SUCCESS IN LIFE

What is the role of beliefs in success and achievements? Norman Vincent Peale in his book, *The Power of Positive Thinking,* was very clear about this issue. According to him, believe in yourself and have faith in your abilities. Without a humble and reasonable confidence in your own powers, you cannot be successful or happy. But with sound self-confidence, you can succeed. Providence plays a vital role in life, but one needs strong faith and belief to sustain what providence has bequeathed us.

Norman Vincent Peale, again, narrates his personal experience with a man who met him after one of his numerous seminars. The man said, "I have terrible disbelief in myself. I have no confidence; I just don't believe I can put it over. I am discouraged and depressed. In fact, I am just about to sink. Here I am, forty years old; why is it that all my life I have been tormented by inferiority feelings, by lack of confidence and by self-doubt?"

It is absolutely safe to say at this point, that the major currency for success is strong belief. The Almighty God has given us all the resources we need to succeed in life. In fact, there is a direct correlation between success, strong self-confidence and confidence in your Maker who has equipped you to succeed. (Deut 8:18). Let us change our lives instantly by changing our beliefs.

SELF-LIMITING BELIEF IS A DISEASE

A self-limiting belief makes someone to lose faith in himself, like the young man mentioned in the story above. Anybody with such belief will remain unproductive, year in, year out. Most times, people attribute their failures to supernatural forces; they do not know that their failures are within them. We are told to have unshakeable belief in our God-given abilities.

SELF-ENHANCING BELIEF: A PANACEA FOR FAILURE

This sort of belief tends to enhance our confidence in our God-given capabilities. It is a necessary ingredient for success. We are enjoined to affirm on daily basis. *"I can do all things through Christ who strengthens me."* For enduring success, we need to be affirmative in our beliefs and hold strongly unto them. To succeed, we must change our beliefs.

HOW POSITIVE BELIEFS AFFECT YOUR LEVEL OF SUCCESS

- It makes you focus on important things in your career.
- It influences how you achieve your goals.
- It helps you cope with the challenges there are.
- It gives you staying power while pursuing success
- It makes you unstoppable.
- The *Law of Attraction* enables you to attract good things into your life.
- It gives supernatural power to conquer.
- The *Law of Accumulation* enables us to believe and accumulate wealth.
- The *Law of Visible Expectation* works here, as we get what we expect.

HOW YOUR BELIEFS AFFECT YOUR BUSINESS DECISIONS

We need to reiterate here that our beliefs come from experiences, parents, society, friends, environment, and childhood. When we believe something to be true, it becomes our reality. Our beliefs affect our business decisions in the following ways:

- It affects the way we delegate duties. If we don't believe in our colleagues, it affects the way we view them and associate with them.
- It affects the way we trust our colleagues with information.
- It affects the way we manage time.
- It affects the way we place others and drive for profitability and growth.
- It influences the way we make our yearly budget and how optimistic/pessimistic we are about our budget.
- It determines whether or not we will get discouraged in driving sales or productivity daily.
- It determines the results we achieve. 2 Chronicles 20:20 says, *"believe in the Lord your God and you shall be established, believe in His prophets and you shall prosper."*

In the face of business downturn, positive beliefs can be re-invigorating, causing things to change for better. The *Law of Sowing and Reaping* will be on hand to generate great performance.

HOW YOUR BELIEF AFFECTS YOUR RELATIONSHIPS

Relationships reflect the bond or connection between two or more persons. Have you not seen some people who deliberately avoid being in contact with other people?

The reason is because their core beliefs impact on their expectations in relationships. People's life experiences and training from childhood help to shape their opinions about themselves, other people and the world they live in.

Basically, our beliefs in relationships come from personal experiences, family expectations and societal beliefs and expectations. If someone has been cheated before in a business deal, he becomes wary of any business proposals. If the religion which one practices, forbids him or her from relating with a group of people, this person may find it impossible to have a relationship with anyone from this group.

NEGATIVE BELIEFS IN RELATIONSHIP

These are stereotypes that we frame based on customs and traditions of people. Examples are:

- ☐ Don't marry from this race; they are bad.
- ☐ Short people are temperamental; avoid them.
- ☐ I only do business with people of my race or tribe or religion.
- ☐ People from this part of the country are dubious.
- ☐ You cannot trust anyone these days.

- ☐ People from this religion are dangerous to deal with.
- ☐ This tribe is known for vices; avoid them.
- ☐ People out there are out to cheat you.

POSITIVE BELIEFS

- ☐ I believe all human beings were created by God.
- ☐ I will love all men and women from all races.
- ☐ I can marry from any tribe.
- ☐ I can build a healthy relationship that can lead to marriage.
- ☐ I can relate with everyone irrespective of tribe and religion.

NEGATIVE BELIEFS AND INTERPRETATION OF EVENTS OF LIFE

The way we interpret things matter so much. Life has been said to be 10% of events and 90% of how we react to the events, or how we interpret the events. Our beliefs affect the way we interpret events, and in the long run, shape our behaviours.

The way we interpret events make these events become realities in our lives. By the *Law of Attraction*, you attract into your life, what you fear or love most. You are what you think every day. People that dread certain things end up attracting them in their lives unknowingly. When we interpret events or circumstances in our own way, either positively or negatively, we tend to attract them to ourselves. This is the way the universe works.

However, there is a solution preferred by William James of Harvard University. He said, *"the greatest discovery of my generation is that a human being can alter his life by altering his attitude."* By the word *attitude*, he refers to what we exhibit and strongly believe in, which propels us to act the way we do. This simply implies that once we interpret events of life positively or monitor our attitude to the events, such situations will automatically change for better in our minds and change our lives positively. Once we assume our interpretation of a situation to be true, it becomes true in our reality by the *Law of Expectation*, which states that *those who expect the best to happen always see the best and verse versa.*

Again, when we interpret things positively, the universe will assist us to make the event a reality. When we hear the symptoms of a pandemic ravaging a nation, we can attract such by wrong interpretation of the event. Do not focus all your energy on interpreting events negatively; don't allow yourself to be a victim of your own interpretation. Remember what Diane Daure said – *"believe something and the universe is on its way to being changed, because you have changed by believing. Once you have changed, other things start to follow".*

In conclusion, let us interpret situations positively and they shall be so. Make excuses for people and you begin to see the good in people and events. For Brian Tracy, positive thinking of events leads to good mental status, health and peak performance. Negative thinking leads to mental illness and decreased effectiveness.

CHAPTER ELEVEN: HOW TO APPLY THE LAW OF BELIEF

"Keep your dreams alive. Understand to achieve anything requires faith and belief in yourself, vision, hard work, determination and dedication. Remember all things are possible for those who believe."

Gail Devers

What is the *Law of Belief?* According to Brian Tracy, whatever you believe strongly, becomes your reality. If you absolutely believe that you are destined to be greatly successful, and you hold on to this belief, no matter what happens, there is nothing in the world that can stop you from becoming successful.

For Tracy, if you absolutely believe that you are a good person with tremendous abilities, and that you are going to do remarkable things with your life, that belief will express itself through all of your actions and will eventually become your reality. You can always feel what your beliefs really are by looking at what you do... you always express your true values in your actions. Thus, the *Law of Belief* says that everything we believe, with strong conviction, becomes true and a reality to us.

Inferring from the above, one can conclude that once we set our minds to do something and have unflinching belief that we can achieve it, it would automatically become our reality. It also means whatever we feel subconsciously as true, long enough, will always manifest itself in the outer world.

The *Law of Attraction* works hand in hand with the *Law of Belief.* The *Law of Attraction* states that whatever we hold in our consciousness, whether desire or other needs, end up becoming our reality. In other words, when we believe strongly in our desires, we literally attract them into our lives.

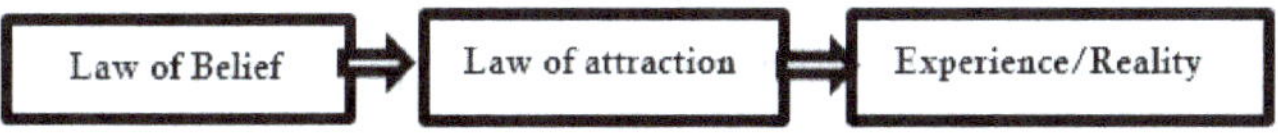

APPLICATION OF THE LAW OF BELIEF

- Replace negative beliefs with positive beliefs.
- Never allow any negative imagination to rest on your mind.
- Use the power of visualization to imagine all the good things you want and believe in them.
- Always remember that God has given you all the resources you need for survival on earth.
- In the face of challenges, stick to your firm belief that God Almighty has destined you to succeed.
- Remember, belief creates reality.

CHAPTER TWELVE: HOW TO REPROGRAMME YOUR BELIEFS

"What distinguishes the majority of men from the few is their ability to act according to their beliefs."

Henry Miller

As a child grows up, he or she learns certain behavioural patterns and beliefs. Automatically, a child is born with a clear slate called the ***Tabula Rasa,*** as propounded by great philosophers over the ages. By the time the child grows up, he or she must have been armed with beliefs to face the world challenges. Tragically, however, much of these beliefs are self-limiting beliefs which the parents and the society must have passed onto the child. The truth is that if the parents always experience a form of phobia, they automatically pass it on to the child. This fear or phobia syndrome will rule the adult life of the person.

Since we know the effects of the environment on our beliefs, it would be very important for us to find out ways we can re-programme our belief system. Mind you, all negative and positive beliefs are embedded in our subconscious minds and they control us.

These beliefs control our behaviours, health, relationships, appetite, self-concept, self-ideal, self-image, mannerism, happiness, etc. The good news is that we can re-programme our beliefs for success.

WAYS TO RE-PROGRAMME OUR BELIEFS

1. Identify all the self-limiting beliefs that held you down over the years.
2. Identify all the self-enhancing beliefs you admire most.
3. Replace the negative beliefs with the positive and self-enhancing beliefs.
4. Create a new self-image you want for yourself.
5. Repeat all the good qualities and beliefs you want to dominate your life.
6. Pray to God to make them a reality on daily basis.
7. Avoid toxic people... remove them from your telephone directory.
8. Identify people that have challenging goals and are focused and make friends with them. Identify with them; study what they did to be successful.
9. Anytime negative thoughts come into your mind, flush them out.
10. Read the bible and other scriptural books for edification.
11. Keep setting big targets for yourself and believe they are achievable.
12. Keep busy; don't be idle.
13. Believe you can do all things through Christ who strengthens you.

CONCLUSION

"Man often becomes what he believes himself to be. If I keep on saying to myself that I cannot do a certain thing, it is possible that I may end up really becoming incapable of doing it. On the contrary, if I shall have the belief that I can do it, I shall surely acquire the capacity to do it, even if I may not have it at the beginning."

Mahatma Gandhi

BELIEFS AND ACTION

Do you want to achieve great success in life? Have you stayed too long on one spot without achieving much? Do you want to change your story? Do you want to enjoy the good things of life?

Please take the following steps:

- ☐ Examine your present beliefs. Are they positive or negative?
- ☐ Are you satisfied with what you have achieved presently? Decide!
- ☐ Change your negative beliefs to positive beliefs.
- ☐ Make new plans to achieve great success.
- ☐ Take action on your plans.
- ☐ Appraise your performance.
- ☐ Refuse to bow down when you face new challenges.
- ☐ Increase your determination and discipline yourself.
- ☐ Pursue your goals to a logical and successful conclusion.

- [ ] Keep changing negative beliefs that may come over your way to positive ones on the road to success.
- [ ] Pray and commit your ways to God Almighty, who is a higher power to guaranty your success.

Finally, remember what Robert Collier has to say:

"Your chances of success in any undertaking can always be measured in your belief in yourself."

Buy Our Books Here:
https://gracelsamson.blogspot.com/

Wisdom-4-Excellence Books *are books that inspire, motivate, educate, recalibrate and resuscitate a Christian's faith in God, and his relationship with Him.*

"UNLOCKING THE POWERS OF YOUR BELIEFS (UTPOYB)" *is the second book in this series. Reading the first book in the series, "The Prayers That Run (TPTR)", will give you a better experience. "Poverty Is A Man (PIAM)" Coming soon, is the third book in this series.*

THE PRAYERS THAT RUN: IS IT FAITH OR FEAR?
In the first two quarters of the year 2020, the human race was petrified by the Covid-19 Pandemic, which infected over ten million people worldwide and claimed over half a million lives. Indeed, the fear was palpable, and Churches which could have been places of solace and refuge were shut down because of the fear of more infections. The panic button of the human race was switched on by the mass media.

Humans grappled with the perplexities that cut across their several dispositions to God, in the aspect of how much He is able to meet their needs. Then suddenly, a book that seeks to recalibrate and resuscitate the praying capacity of Christians came out of the blues. This eye-opening book reveals the secrets on how we can get our prayers running to GOD with faith, rather than running to the devil with fear.

The author explains the distinguishing factors one must possess to attract God's unlimited grace. The book makes you appreciate your tripatriach nature and totally disregard the lopsided Christianity that unfortunately, many practice. This book encapsulates all aspects of life, while capitalising on our motives, intentions, lifestyle and relationship with God through prayers. It will empower you to be a shining light and a power-filled Christian that uses affliction as tool for greatness, rather than a tool for despair.

****

UNLOCKING THE POWERS OF YOUR BELIEFS *(<u>UTPOYB</u>): With several practical theories related to belief, this book deals extensively on the matter of belief, as it relates to human productivity.*

Written by seasoned authors, the book will transform your belief system from whatever level it is now, to at least a 95% level. It is an eye-opener, that will throw more enlightenment to you on how to harness the potentials of your belief system, to achieve great success in life. The exposition in this book is truly unbelievable and if you to read it till the end, you will learn how to transform your life, by transforming your belief.

Begin to UNLOCK THE POWERS OF YOUR BELIEFS now!!!

****

POVERTY IS A MAN: PERHAPS A WOMAN (<u>PIAM</u>):
You do not need to work too hard before you can make it in life, all you need is to be DILLIGENT, so that you are prepared for your CHANCE, when your TIME comes.

The extent to which you believe in your power to exercise your God given dominion and authority, that is the extent you will reach, and that is "how rich" or "how successful" you will eventually become.

"POVERTY IS A MAN: PERHAPS A WOMAN", treats **POVERTY** *as a man or even a woman because they are the only creatures of God with an ordination. If you wish to know more about the ordination, then read on!!!!!!!!!!!!!!!!*

EPILOGUE

Why do some people enjoy life to the fullest, while millions of others live unfulfilled dreams, with too many regrets that perpetually keep them unhappy and full of bitterness about life? Why do some people believe that the beautiful things of the world such as lovely families, choice cars, houses, good paying jobs, good health, wonderful relationships, etc, are not for them but for a selected few?

The reason is simple. The people that enjoy life have beneficial beliefs that empower them to accomplish great feats and outstanding achievements. The other people who perform poorly, have over the years failed to acknowledge the power of their beliefs. They have non-beneficial beliefs.

It is so disheartening that millions all over the world have the wrong set of beliefs that keep them in bondage. "Unlocking the Powers of Your Beliefs" was written to encourage us to exploit the powers in our beliefs. When we believe we can move mountains and don't doubt it, life becomes sweet and achievements become very easy. This book is refreshing and powerful. It will teach you everything you need to know about beliefs, and how to use them to your advantage in life.

ABOUT THE AUTHORS

Mr **Jude Okey Dike** is an accountant by profession and a fellow of the Institute of Chartered Accountants of Nigeria (ICAN). He has worked for over two decades in one of the most reputable banks in Nigeria and has risen to the enviable position of a Regional Manager. He likes reading and motivating people around him to reach the zenith of their aspirations in life. He is married to his beautiful wife, Chinwe Dike, and blessed with wonderful children.

Dr **Grace L. Samson** is an academician, researcher, motivational speaker and a preacher and lover of the gospel of Christ. She obtained her doctorate degree in Advanced Computer and Informatics from the University of Huddersfield, in the United Kingdom.